chicken **dishes**

Easy dishes to cook at home

This edition published in 2010
LOVE FOOD is an imprint of Parragon Books Ltd

Parragon
Queen Street House
4 Queen Street
Bath BA1 1HE, UK

ISBN: 978-1-4075-8101-9

Printed in China

Designed by Talking Design
Cover and introduction text by Frances Eames

Notes for the Reader
This book uses imperial, metric, and US cup measurements. Follow the same units of measurement throughout; do not mix imperial and metric. All spoon measurements are level: teaspoons are assumed to be 5 ml, and tablespoons are assumed to be 15 ml. Unless otherwise stated, milk is assumed to be whole, eggs and individual vegetables such as potatoes are medium, and pepper is freshly ground black pepper.

The times given are an approximate guide only. Preparation times differ according to the techniques used by different people and the cooking times may also vary from those given as a result of the type of oven used. Optional ingredients, variations or serving suggestions have not been included in the calculations.

Recipes using raw or very lightly cooked eggs should be avoided by infants, the elderly, pregnant women, convalescents, and anyone with a chronic condition. Pregnant and breastfeeding women are advised to avoid eating peanuts and peanut products. Sufferers from nut allergies should be aware that some of the ready-prepared ingredients used in the recipes in this book may contain nuts. Always check the packaging before use.

Contents

introduction

Every once in a while it is good to acknowledge one of the mainstays of our diet. This book provides the opportunity to celebrate chicken in all its tasty guises.

Chicken is one of the unsung heroes of our daily diet. It is healthy, easy to cook, and wonderfully versatile. In a world of fad diets it is refreshing to know that the majority of meateaters are happy to eat chicken. Chicken has amazing appeal and can be adapted to a multitude of flavors, cuisines, and occasions. Chicken dishes are suitable for family meals or entertaining all year round. You can match chicken recipes with fresh seasonal vegetables for the best flavors and colors. Try cooking a comforting chicken casserole to brighten up a winter's day, or serve up a crisp chicken salad in the summer with a glass of chilled white wine. You can even barbecue with chicken wings or thighs. From pasta and rice dishes to roasts and curries, good-quality chicken really is the linchpin of wholesome, healthy eating.

Buying Chicken

All good supermarkets and butchers sell several different cuts of chicken—choose from breast, leg, thigh or wing, either with or without bones or skin. Golden crispy chicken skin is always popular, but do remember that it is high in fat. It is usually more economical to buy a whole chicken and joint it yourself. A whole chicken can feed a family over a few meals, especially if you boil the carcass to make stock. It is always worth buying the best quality chicken you can afford as it will have a better flavor.

Cooking Tips

Chicken dishes are quick, easy, low-fat, and universally popular. However, if chicken is not cooked properly, it can have a tendency toward being dry, tough, and stringy. So what are the best ways of cooking it so you end up with moist, tender, and flavorful meat? There are two basic methods for cooking: dry heat and moist heat. Dry heat methods include baking, roasting, broiling, and sautéing, while examples of moist heat methods are poaching, steaming, and slow cooking. When cooking chicken breasts with dry heat, use high heat and cook for a short period of time. When using moist heat, use low heat and cook for a slightly longer period of time.

Timings

Chicken breasts have little connective tissue which means that that they can be cooked quickly. However, they also have little fat, which means they can become dry if cooked too long.

As a general guide:

- Broiled chicken breasts cook in 8–10 minutes
- Poached chicken breasts cook in about 15 minutes

When cooking with dry heat, it is a good idea to pound the chicken breasts to an equal thickness so they will cook evenly. Remember that the meat will continue to cook after it is removed from the heat; the internal temperature will rise slightly in the first few minutes it is off the heat.

Safety Tips

While some meats can be served medium rare, or even rare, chicken must be cooked thoroughly to eliminate any bacteria. To test whether chicken is cooked, insert a skewer into the thickest part of the meat; if the juices run clear, it is safe to eat. Alternatively, cut the chicken breast in half to make sure that no traces of pink remain. If you have young children, elderly persons, or those with a compromised immune system in your household, you may prefer to use a meat thermometer to check the internal temperature. Always store raw and cooked chicken separately in the refrigerator. Make sure that any raw chicken is placed on the lowest shelf to prevent it leaking on any food on the lower shelves. Make sure to wash your hands after handling raw chicken to prevent cross-contamination.

simple **soups**

Cream of Chicken
Soup

SERVES 4

3 tbsp butter
4 shallots, chopped
1 leek, sliced
1 lb/450 g skinless chicken breasts, chopped
2½ cups chicken stock
1 tbsp chopped fresh parsley
1 tbsp chopped fresh thyme, plus extra sprigs to garnish
¾ cup heavy cream
salt and pepper

Melt the butter in a large pan over medium heat. Add the shallots and cook, stirring, for 3 minutes, until slightly softened. Add the leek and cook for another 5 minutes, stirring. Add the chicken, stock, and herbs, and season with salt and pepper. Bring to a boil, then lower the heat and simmer for 25 minutes, until the chicken is tender and cooked through. Remove from the heat and let cool for 10 minutes.

Transfer the soup into a food processor or blender and process until smooth (you may need to do this in batches). Return the soup to the rinsed-out pan and warm over low heat for 5 minutes.

Stir in the cream and cook for another 2 minutes, then remove from the heat and ladle into serving bowls. Garnish with sprigs of thyme and serve immediately.

Chicken Noodle
Soup

SERVES 4–6

- 2 skinless chicken breasts
- 5 cups water or chicken stock
- 3 carrots, peeled and cut into ¼-inch/5-mm slices
- 3 oz/85 g vermicelli (or other small noodles)
- salt and pepper
- fresh tarragon leaves, to garnish

Place the chicken breasts in a large saucepan, add the water, and bring to a simmer. Cook for 25–30 minutes. Skim any foam from the surface, if necessary. Remove the chicken from the stock and keep warm.

Continue to simmer the stock, add the carrots and vermicelli, and cook for 4–5 minutes.

Thinly slice or shred the chicken breasts and place in warmed serving dishes.

Season the soup to taste with salt and pepper and pour over the chicken. Serve immediately garnished with the tarragon.

Thai Chicken
Soup

SERVES 4

1 tbsp sesame oil or chili oil
2 garlic cloves, chopped
2 scallions, trimmed and sliced
1 leek, trimmed and finely sliced
1 tbsp grated fresh ginger
1 red chile, seeded and finely chopped
12 oz/350 g skinless, boneless chicken breasts, cut into strips
scant 3½ cups chicken stock
2 tbsp rice wine
1 tbsp chopped lemongrass
6 kaffir lime leaves, finely shredded
7 oz/200 g fine egg noodles
salt and pepper

Heat the oil in a wok or large pan. Add the garlic and cook over medium heat, stirring, for 1 minute, then add the scallions, leek, ginger, and chile and cook, stirring, for another 3 minutes. Add the chicken, stock, and rice wine, bring to a boil, and simmer for 20 minutes. Stir in the lemongrass and lime leaves.

Bring a separate pan of water to a boil and add the noodles. Cook for 3 minutes, drain well, then add them to the soup. Season to taste with salt and pepper. Cook for another 2 minutes. Remove from the heat, ladle into warmed serving bowls, and serve hot.

Chicken & Broccoli
Soup

SERVES 4–6

8 oz/225 g head of broccoli
4 tbsp unsalted butter
1 onion, chopped
generous 1/8 cup basmati rice
8 oz/225 g skinless, boneless chicken breast, cut into thin slivers
scant 1/4 cup all-purpose whole wheat flour
1 1/4 cups milk
2 cups chicken stock
generous 1/3 cup corn kernels
salt and pepper

Break the broccoli into small florets and cook in a pan of lightly salted boiling water for 3 minutes, drain, then plunge into cold water and set aside.

Melt the butter in a pan over medium heat, add the onion, rice, and chicken, and cook for 5 minutes, stirring frequently.

Remove the pan from the heat and stir in the flour. Return to the heat and cook for 2 minutes, stirring constantly. Stir in the milk and then the stock. Bring to a boil, stirring constantly, then reduce the heat and let simmer for 10 minutes.

Drain the broccoli and add to the pan with the corn and salt and pepper to taste. Let simmer for 5 minutes, or until the rice is tender, then serve.

Chicken & Rice
Soup

SERVES 4

6¼ cups chicken stock
2 small carrots, very thinly sliced
1 celery stalk, finely diced
1 baby leek, halved lengthwise and thinly sliced
1 cup petit pois, defrosted if frozen
1 cup cooked rice
5½ oz/150 g cooked chicken, sliced
2 tsp chopped fresh tarragon
1 tbsp chopped fresh parsley
salt and pepper
sprigs of fresh parsley, to garnish

Put the stock in a large saucepan and add the carrots, celery, and leek. Bring to a boil, reduce the heat to low, and simmer gently, partially covered, for 10 minutes.

Stir in the petit pois, rice, and chicken and continue cooking for an additional 10–15 minutes, or until the vegetables are tender.

Add the chopped tarragon and parsley, then taste and adjust the seasoning, adding salt and pepper as needed.

Ladle the soup into warmed bowls, garnish with parsley, and serve.

Chicken Gumbo

Soup

SERVES 6

- 2 tbsp olive oil
- 4 tbsp all-purpose flour
- 1 onion, finely chopped
- 1 small green bell pepper, seeded and finely chopped
- 1 celery stalk, finely chopped
- 5 cups chicken stock
- 14 oz/400 g canned chopped tomatoes
- 3 garlic cloves, finely chopped or crushed
- 4½ oz/125 g okra, stems removed, cut into ¼-inch/5-mm thick slices
- 4 tbsp white rice
- 7 oz/200 g cooked chicken, cubed
- 4 oz/115 g cooked garlic sausage, sliced or cubed
- salt and pepper

Heat the oil in a large, heavy-bottom saucepan over medium–high and stir in the flour. Cook for about 15 minutes, stirring occasionally, until the mixture is a rich golden brown.

Add the onion, green bell pepper, and celery and continue cooking for about 10 minutes until the onion softens.

Slowly pour in the stock and bring to a boil, stirring well and scraping the bottom of the pan to mix in the flour. Remove the pan from the heat.

Add the tomatoes and garlic. Stir in the okra and rice and season to taste with salt and pepper. Reduce the heat, cover, and simmer for 20 minutes, or until the okra is tender.

Add the chicken and sausage and continue simmering for about 10 minutes. Taste and adjust the seasoning, if necessary, and ladle into warmed bowls to serve.

Thai Chicken-Coconut *Soup*

SERVES 4

4 oz/115 g dried cellophane noodles
5 cups chicken or vegetable stock
1 lemongrass stalk, crushed
½-inch/1-cm piece fresh ginger, peeled and very finely chopped
2 fresh kaffir lime leaves, thinly sliced
1 fresh red chile, or to taste, seeded and thinly sliced
2 skinless, boneless chicken breasts, thinly sliced
scant 1 cup coconut cream
2 tbsp nam pla (Thai fish sauce)
1 tbsp fresh lime juice
scant ½ cup bean sprouts
4 scallions, green part only, finely sliced
fresh cilantro leaves, to garnish

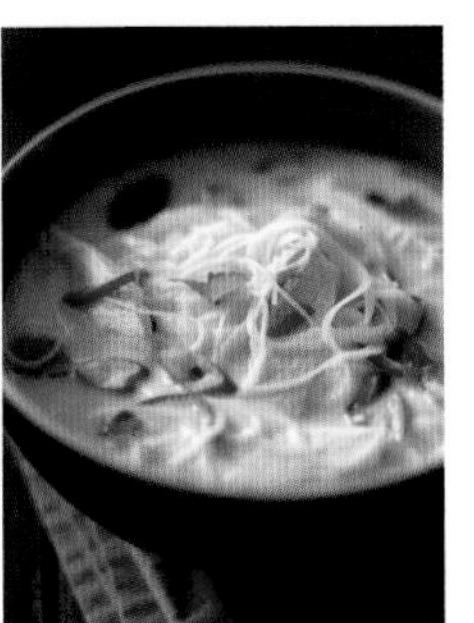

Soak the dried noodles in a large bowl with enough lukewarm water to cover for 20 minutes, until soft. Alternatively, cook according to the package instructions. Drain well and set aside.

Meanwhile, bring the stock to a boil in a large pan over high heat. Lower the heat, add the lemongrass, ginger, kaffir lime leaves, and chile and simmer for 5 minutes. Add the chicken and continue simmering for an additional 3 minutes, or until cooked. Stir in the coconut cream, nam pla, and lime juice and continue simmering for 3 minutes. Add the bean sprouts and scallions and simmer for an additional 1 minute. Taste and gradually add extra nam pla or lime juice at this point, if needed. Remove and discard the lemongrass stalk.

Divide the noodles among 4 bowls. Bring the soup back to a boil, then ladle into the bowls. The heat of the soup will warm the noodles. To garnish, sprinkle with cilantro leaves.

the **classics**

Roast
Chicken

SERVES 6

- 1 free-range chicken, weighing 5 lb/2.25 kg
- 4 tbsp butter
- 2 tbsp chopped fresh lemon thyme
- 1 lemon, quartered
- ½ cup white wine
- salt and pepper
- 6 fresh thyme sprigs, for garnish

Preheat the oven to 425°F/220°C. Make sure the chicken is clean, wiping it inside and out using paper towels, and place in a roasting pan.

Place the butter in a bowl and soften with a fork, then mix in the thyme and season well with salt and pepper. Butter the chicken all over with the herb butter, inside and out, and place the lemon quarters inside the body cavity. Pour the wine over the chicken.

Roast the chicken in the center of the oven for 20 minutes. Reduce the temperature to 375°F/190°C and continue to roast for an additional 1¼ hours, basting frequently. Cover with foil if the skin starts to brown too much. If the pan dries out, add a little more wine or water.

Test that the chicken is cooked by piercing the thickest part of the leg with a sharp knife or skewer and making sure the juices run clear. Remove from the oven.

Remove the chicken from the roasting pan and place on a warmed serving plate to rest, covered with foil, for 10 minutes before carving.

Place the roasting pan on the top of the stove and bubble the pan juices gently over low heat until they have reduced and are thick and glossy. Season to taste with salt and pepper. Serve the chicken with the pan juices and sprinkle with the thyme sprigs.

Chicken, Potato & Leek Pie

SERVES 4

- 8 oz/225 g waxy potatoes, cubed
- 5 tbsp butter
- 1 skinless, boneless chicken breast, about 6 oz/175 g, cubed
- 1 leek, sliced
- 2 cups sliced crimini mushrooms
- 2½ tbsp all-purpose flour
- 1¼ cups milk
- 1 tbsp whole grain mustard
- 2 tbsp chopped fresh sage
- 8 oz/225 g filo dough, thawed if frozen
- 3 tbsp melted butter
- salt and pepper

Cook the potato cubes in a pan of boiling water for 5 minutes. Drain and set aside.

Melt the butter in a skillet and cook the chicken cubes for 5 minutes or until browned all over.

Add the leek and mushrooms and cook for 3 minutes, stirring. Stir in the flour and cook for 1 minute stirring constantly. Gradually stir in the milk and bring to a boil. Add the mustard, sage, potato cubes and salt and pepper and simmer for 10 minutes.

Meanwhile, line a deep pie dish with half of the sheets of filo dough. Spoon the sauce into the dish and cover with 1 sheet of dough. Brush the dough with melted butter and lay another sheet on top. Brush this sheet with butter.

Cut the remaining filo dough into strips and fold them onto the top of the pie to create a ruffled effect. Brush the strips with the melted butter and cook in a preheated oven, 350°F/180°C, for 45 minutes or until golden brown and crisp. Serve hot.

Coq
au Vin

SERVES 4

1/4 cup butter
2 tbsp olive oil
4 lb/1.8 kg chicken pieces
4 oz/115 g rindless smoked bacon, cut into strips
4 oz/115 g pearl onions, peeled
4 oz/115 g cremini mushrooms, halved
2 garlic cloves, finely chopped
2 tbsp brandy
scant 1 cup red wine
1 1/4 cups chicken stock
1 bouquet garni
2 tbsp all-purpose flour
salt and pepper
bay leaves, to garnish

Melt half the butter with the olive oil in a large, flameproof casserole. Add the chicken and cook over medium heat, stirring, for 8–10 minutes, or until golden brown. Add the bacon, onions, mushrooms, and garlic.

Pour in the brandy and set it alight with a match or taper. When the flames have died down, add the wine, stock, and bouquet garni and season to taste with salt and pepper. Bring to a boil, reduce the heat, and simmer gently for 1 hour, or until the chicken pieces are cooked through and tender. Meanwhile, make a beurre manié by mashing the remaining butter with the flour in a small bowl.

Remove and discard the bouquet garni. Transfer the chicken to a large plate and keep warm. Stir the beurre manié into the casserole, a little at a time. Bring to a boil, return the chicken to the casserole, and serve immediately, garnished with bay leaves.

Jerk Chicken

SERVES 4

- 2 red chiles
- 2 tbsp corn oil, plus extra for brushing
- 2 garlic cloves, finely chopped
- 1 tbsp finely chopped onion
- 1 tbsp finely chopped scallion
- 1 tbsp white wine vinegar
- 1 tbsp lime juice
- 2 tsp raw brown sugar
- 1 tsp dried thyme
- 1 tsp ground cinnamon
- 1 tsp ground allspice
- 1/4 tsp freshly grated nutmeg
- 4 chicken quarters
- salt and pepper
- sprigs of fresh cilantro and lime wedges, to garnish

Seed and finely chop the red chiles, then place them in a small glass bowl with the oil, garlic, onion, scallion, vinegar, lime juice, raw brown sugar, thyme, cinnamon, allspice, and nutmeg. Season to taste with salt and pepper and mash thoroughly with a fork.

Using a sharp knife, make a series of diagonal slashes in the chicken pieces and place them in a large, shallow, nonmetallic dish. Spoon the jerk seasoning over the chicken, rubbing it well into the slashes. Cover and let marinate in the refrigerator for up to 8 hours.

Preheat the broiler. Remove the chicken from the marinade, discarding the marinade, brush with oil and cook under the preheated broiler, turning frequently, for 30–35 minutes. Transfer to plates and serve garnished with sprigs of cilantro and lime wedges.

Sweet & Sour
Chicken

SERVES 4–6

4 skinless, boneless chicken breasts
½ cup all-purpose flour
2 tbsp olive oil
2 large garlic cloves, chopped
1 bay leaf
1 tbsp grated fresh ginger
1 tbsp chopped fresh lemongrass
4 tbsp sherry vinegar
5 tbsp rice wine or sherry
1 tbsp honey
1 tsp chili powder
½ cup orange juice
4 tbsp lime juice
salt and pepper
wedges of lime, to garnish
freshly cooked noodles, to serve

Season the chicken breasts on both sides with salt and pepper to taste, then roll them in the flour until coated. Heat the oil in a large skillet. Add the garlic and cook, stirring, over medium heat for 1 minute. Add the chicken, bay leaf, ginger, and lemongrass and cook for 2 minutes on each side.

Add the vinegar, rice wine, and honey, bring to a boil, then lower the heat and simmer, stirring occasionally, for 10 minutes. Add the chili powder, then stir in the orange juice and lime juice. Simmer for another 10 minutes. Using a perforated spoon, lift out the chicken and set aside. Strain and reserve the liquid and discard the bay leaf, then return the liquid to the pan with the chicken. Simmer for another 15–20 minutes.

Remove from the heat and transfer to individual serving plates. Serve with freshly cooked noodles and garnish with lime wedges.

The Ultimate
Chicken Burger

SERVES 4

4 large skinless, boneless chicken breasts
1 large egg white
1 tbsp cornstarch
1 tbsp all-purpose flour
1 egg, beaten
1 cup fresh white breadcrumbs
2 tbsp corn oil
2 beefsteak tomatoes, sliced

To serve

4 burger buns, sliced
shredded lettuce
mayonnaise

Place the chicken breasts between 2 sheets of nonstick parchment paper and flatten slightly using a meat mallet or a rolling pin. Beat the egg white and cornstarch together, then brush over the chicken. Cover and let chill for 30 minutes, then coat in the flour.

Place the egg and breadcrumbs in 2 separate bowls and coat the burgers first in the egg, allowing any excess to drip back into the bowl, then in the breadcrumbs.

Heat a heavy-bottom skillet and add the oil. When hot, add the burgers and cook over medium heat for 6–8 minutes on each side, or until thoroughly cooked. If you are in doubt, it is worth cutting one of the burgers in half. If there is any sign of pinkness, cook for a little longer. Add the tomato slices for the last 1–2 minutes of the cooking time to heat through.

Serve the burgers in the burger buns with the tomato slices, a little shredded lettuce and a spoonful of mayonnaise.

perfect **pasta**

Spaghetti with *Parsley Chicken*

SERVES 4

1 tbsp olive oil
thinly pared rind of 1 lemon, cut into julienne strips
1 tsp finely chopped fresh ginger
1 tsp sugar
1 cup chicken stock
9 oz/250 g dried spaghetti
4 tbsp butter
8 oz/225 g skinless, boneless chicken breasts, diced
1 red onion, finely chopped
leaves from 2 bunches of flat-leaf parsley
salt

Heat the olive oil in a heavy-bottom pan. Add the lemon rind and cook over low heat, stirring frequently, for 5 minutes. Stir in the ginger and sugar, season to taste with salt, and cook, stirring constantly, for an additional 2 minutes. Pour in the chicken stock, bring to a boil, then cook for 5 minutes, or until the liquid has reduced by half.

Meanwhile, bring a large, heavy-bottom pan of lightly salted water to a boil. Add the pasta, return to a boil, and cook for 8–10 minutes, or until tender but still firm to the bite.

Melt half the butter in a skillet. Add the chicken and onion and cook, stirring frequently, for 5 minutes, or until the chicken is lightly browned all over. Stir in the lemon and ginger mixture and cook for 1 minute. Stir in the parsley leaves and cook, stirring constantly, for an additional 3 minutes.

Drain the pasta and transfer to a warmed serving dish, then add the remaining butter and toss well. Add the chicken sauce, toss again, and serve.

Pappardelle with Chicken & Porcini

SERVES 4

- 3/8 cup dried porcini mushrooms
- 3/4 cup hot water
- 1 lb 12 oz/800 g canned chopped tomatoes
- 1 fresh red chile, seeded and finely chopped
- 3 tbsp olive oil
- 12 oz/350 g skinless, boneless chicken, cut into thin strips
- 2 garlic cloves, finely chopped
- 12 oz/350 g dried pappardelle
- salt and pepper
- 2 tbsp chopped fresh flat-leaf parsley, to garnish

Place the porcini in a small bowl, add the hot water, and let soak for 20 minutes. Meanwhile, place the tomatoes and their can juices in a heavy-bottom pan and break them up with a wooden spoon, then stir in the chile. Bring to a boil, reduce the heat, and simmer, stirring occasionally, for 30 minutes, or until reduced.

Remove the mushrooms from their soaking liquid with a slotted spoon, reserving the liquid. Strain the liquid through a coffee filter paper or cheesecloth-lined strainer into the tomatoes and simmer for an additional 15 minutes.

Meanwhile, heat 2 tablespoons of the olive oil in a heavy-bottom skillet. Add the chicken and cook, stirring frequently, until golden brown all over and tender. Stir in the mushrooms and garlic and cook for 5 minutes.

While the chicken is cooking, bring a large, heavy-bottom pan of lightly salted water to a boil. Add the pasta, return to a boil, and cook for 8–10 minutes, or until tender but still firm to the bite. Drain well, transfer to a warmed serving dish, drizzle with the remaining olive oil, and toss lightly. Stir the chicken mixture into the tomato sauce, season to taste with salt and pepper, and spoon onto the pasta. Toss lightly, sprinkle with parsley, and serve immediately.

Penne with
Chicken & Feta

SERVES 4

- 2 tbsp olive oil
- 1 lb/450 g skinless, boneless chicken breasts, cut into thin strips
- 6 scallions, chopped
- 8 oz/225 g feta cheese, diced
- 4 tbsp snipped fresh chives
- 1 lb/450 g dried penne
- salt and pepper

Heat the olive oil in a heavy-bottom skillet. Add the chicken and cook over medium heat, stirring frequently, for 5–8 minutes, or until golden all over and cooked through. Add the scallions and cook for 2 minutes. Stir the feta cheese into the skillet with half the chives and season to taste with salt and pepper.

Meanwhile, bring a large, heavy-bottom pan of lightly salted water to a boil. Add the pasta, return to a boil, and cook for 8–10 minutes, or until tender but still firm to the bite. Drain well, then transfer to a warmed serving dish.

Spoon the chicken mixture onto the pasta, toss lightly, and serve immediately, garnished with the remaining chives.

Fettuccine with Chicken & Onion Cream Sauce

SERVES 4

1 tbsp olive oil
2 tbsp butter
1 garlic clove, very finely chopped
4 skinless, boneless chicken breasts
1 onion, chopped finely
1 chicken bouillon cube, crumbled
½ cup water
1¼ cups heavy cream
¾ cup milk
6 scallions, green part included, sliced diagonally
⅓ cup freshly grated Parmesan
1 lb/450 g dried fettuccine
salt and pepper
chopped fresh flat-leaf parsley, to garnish

Heat the oil and butter with the garlic in a large skillet over medium–low heat. Cook the garlic until just beginning to color. Add the chicken and raise the heat to medium. Cook for 4–5 minutes on each side, or until the juices are no longer pink. Season to taste with salt and pepper. Remove from the heat. Remove the chicken, leaving the oil in the skillet. Slice the chicken diagonally into thin strips and set aside.

Reheat the oil in the skillet. Add the onion and gently cook for 5 minutes, or until soft. Add the crumbled bouillon cube and the water. Bring to a boil, then simmer over medium–low heat for 10 minutes. Stir in the cream, milk, scallions, and Parmesan. Simmer until heated through and slightly thickened.

Meanwhile, bring a large saucepan of lightly salted water to a boil. Add the pasta, bring back to a boil, and cook for 8–10 minutes, or until tender but still firm to the bite. Drain and transfer to a warmed serving dish. Layer the chicken slices over the pasta. Pour over the sauce, then garnish with parsley and serve.

Farfalle with Chicken & Broccoli

SERVES 4

4 tbsp olive oil
5 tbsp butter
3 garlic cloves, very finely chopped
1 lb/450 g boneless, skinless chicken breasts, diced
1/4 tsp dried chile flakes
1 lb/450 g small broccoli florets
10 1/2 oz/300 g dried farfalle (pasta bows)
6 oz/175 g bottled roasted red bell peppers, drained and diced
1 cup chicken stock
salt and pepper

Bring a large pan of salted water to a boil. Meanwhile, heat the olive oil and butter in a large skillet over medium–low heat. Add the garlic and cook until just beginning to color. Add the diced chicken, then raise the heat to medium and cook for 4–5 minutes, or until the chicken is no longer pink. Add the chile flakes and season to taste with salt and pepper. Remove from the heat.

Plunge the broccoli into the boiling water and cook for 2 minutes. Remove with a slotted spoon and set aside. Bring the water back to a boil. Add the pasta and cook for 8–10 minutes, or until tender but still firm to the bite. Drain and add to the chicken mixture in the pan. Add the broccoli and roasted bell peppers. Pour in the stock. Simmer briskly over medium–high heat, stirring frequently, until most of the liquid has been absorbed.

Transfer to warmed dishes and serve.

Fettuccine with
Chicken & Basil Pesto

SERVES 4

2 tbsp vegetable oil
4 skinless, boneless chicken breasts
12 oz/350 g dried fettuccine
salt and pepper
sprig of fresh basil, to garnish

Pesto

1⅔ cups shredded fresh basil
½ cup extra virgin olive oil
3 tbsp pine nuts
3 garlic cloves, crushed
½ cup freshly grated Parmesan cheese
2 tbsp freshly grated Romano cheese
salt

To make the pesto, put the basil, olive oil, pine nuts, garlic, and a generous pinch of salt in a food processor or blender. Process the ingredients until smooth. Scrape the mixture into a bowl and stir in the cheeses.

Heat the vegetable oil in a skillet over medium heat. Cook the chicken breasts, turning once, for 8–10 minutes, or until the juices are no longer pink. Cut into small cubes.

Meanwhile, bring a large saucepan of lightly salted water to a boil. Add the pasta, bring back to a boil, and cook for 8–10 minutes, or until tender but still firm to the bite. Drain and transfer to a warmed serving dish. Add the chicken and pesto, then season with pepper. Toss well to mix.

Garnish with a sprig of basil and serve warm.

a little **bit of luxury**

Chicken Liver Pâté
with Marsala

SERVES 4–6

1 cup butter
8 oz/225 g trimmed chicken livers, thawed if frozen
2 tbsp Marsala or brandy
1½ tsp chopped fresh sage
1 garlic clove, coarsely chopped
⅔ cup heavy cream
salt and pepper
fresh bay leaves or sage leaves, for garnish
crackers, for serving

Melt 3 tablespoons of the butter in a large, heavy-bottom skillet. Add the chicken livers and cook over medium heat for about 4 minutes on each side. They should be browned on the outside but still pink in the middle. Transfer to a food processor and process until finely chopped.

Stir the Marsala or brandy into the skillet, scraping up any sediment with a wooden spoon, then add to the food processor with the sage, garlic, and ½ cup of the remaining butter. Process until smooth. Add the cream, season with salt and pepper, and process until thoroughly combined and smooth. Spoon the pâté into a dish or individual ramekins, level the surface, and let cool completely.

Melt the remaining butter, then spoon it over the surface of the pâté. Decorate with herb leaves, cool, then let chill in the refrigerator. Serve with crackers.

Smoked Chicken & *Cranberry Salad*

SERVES 4

1 smoked chicken, weighing 3 lb/1.3 kg
scant 1 cup dried cranberries
2 tbsp apple juice or water
7 oz/200 g sugar snap peas
2 ripe avocados
juice of ½ lemon
4 lettuce hearts
1 bunch watercress, trimmed
2 oz/55 g arugula

Dressing

2 tbsp olive oil
1 tbsp walnut oil
2 tbsp lemon juice
1 tbsp chopped fresh mixed herbs, such as parsley and lemon thyme
salt and pepper

Carve the chicken carefully, slicing the white meat. Divide the legs into thighs and drumsticks and trim the wings. Cover with plastic wrap and refrigerate.

Put the cranberries in a bowl. Stir in the apple juice, then cover with plastic wrap and let soak for 30 minutes.

Meanwhile, blanch the sugar snap peas, then refresh under cold running water and drain.

Peel, pit, and slice the avocados and toss in the lemon juice to prevent discoloration.

Separate the lettuce hearts and arrange on a large serving platter with the avocados, sugar snap peas, watercress, arugula, and the chicken.

Put all the dressing ingredients, with salt and pepper to taste, in a screw-top jar, then screw on the lid and shake until well blended.

Drain the cranberries and mix them with the dressing, then pour over the salad. Serve immediately.

Thai-style Chicken
Salad

SERVES 4

14 oz/400 g small new potatoes, scrubbed and cut in half, lengthwise
7 oz/200 g baby corn cobs
1½ cups bean sprouts
3 scallions, trimmed and sliced
4 cooked, skinless chicken breasts, sliced
1 tbsp chopped lemongrass
2 tbsp chopped fresh cilantro
salt and pepper
wedges of lime, to garnish
fresh cilantro leaves, to garnish

Dressing

6 tbsp chili oil or sesame oil
2 tbsp lime juice
1 tbsp light soy sauce
1 tbsp chopped fresh cilantro
1 small red chile, seeded and finely sliced

Bring two pans of water to a boil. Put the potatoes into one pan and cook for 15 minutes until tender. Put the corn cobs into the other pan and cook for 5 minutes until tender. Drain the potatoes and corn cobs well and let cool.

When the vegetables are cool, transfer them into a large serving dish. Add the bean sprouts, scallions, chicken, lemongrass, and cilantro and season with salt and pepper.

To make the dressing, put all the ingredients into a screw-top jar and shake well. Alternatively, put them into a bowl and mix together well. Drizzle the dressing over the salad and garnish with lime wedges and cilantro leaves. Serve at once.

Roast Chicken Salad
with Pesto Cream

SERVES 4–6

1 lb 5 oz/600 g cooked boneless chicken, any skin removed and cut into bite-size chunks
3 celery sticks, chopped
2 large skinned red bell peppers from a jar, well drained and sliced
salt and pepper
iceberg lettuce leaves, to serve

Pesto cream

5 oz/150 ml sour cream
about 4 tbsp bottled pesto sauce

To make the pesto cream, put the sour cream into a large bowl, then beat in 4 tablespoons pesto sauce. Taste and add more pesto if you want a stronger flavor.

Add the chicken, celery, and bell peppers to the bowl and gently toss together. Add salt and pepper to taste and toss again. Cover and chill until required.

Remove the salad from the refrigerator 10 minutes before serving to return to room temperature. Give the salad ingredients a good stir, then divide among individual plates lined with lettuce leaves.

Thai Red Chicken
Curry

SERVES 2–4

6 garlic cloves, chopped
2 fresh red chiles, chopped
2 tbsp chopped fresh lemongrass
1 tsp finely grated lime zest
1 tbsp chopped fresh kaffir lime leaves
1 tbsp Thai red curry paste
1 tbsp coriander seeds, toasted and crushed
1 tbsp chili oil
4 skinless, boneless chicken breasts, sliced
1¼ cups coconut milk
1¼ cups chicken stock
1 tbsp soy sauce
⅓ cup shelled unsalted peanuts, toasted and ground
3 scallions, diagonally sliced
1 red bell pepper, seeded and sliced
3 Thai eggplants, sliced
2 tbsp chopped fresh Thai basil or fresh cilantro
1–2 tbsp chopped fresh cilantro, to garnish
freshly cooked jasmine rice, to serve

Place the garlic, chiles, lemongrass, lime zest, kaffir lime leaves, curry paste, and coriander seeds in a food processor and process until the mixture is smooth.

Heat the oil in a preheated wok or large skillet over high heat. Add the chicken and the garlic mixture and stir-fry for 5 minutes. Add the coconut milk, stock, and soy sauce and bring to a boil. Reduce the heat and cook, stirring, for an additional 3 minutes. Stir in the ground peanuts and simmer for 20 minutes.

Add the scallions, bell pepper, and eggplants and simmer, stirring occasionally, for an additional 10 minutes. Remove from the heat, stir in the basil, and garnish with cilantro. Serve immediately with freshly cooked jasmine rice.

Chicken
Biryani

SERVES 8

- 1½ tsp finely chopped fresh ginger
- 1½ tsp crushed garlic
- 1 tbsp garam masala
- 1 tsp chili powder
- 2 tsp salt
- 1¼ cups plain yogurt
- 5 crushed cardamom pods
- 3 lb 5 oz/1.5 kg chicken
- ⅔ cup milk
- 1 tsp saffron strands
- 6 tbsp ghee
- 2 onions, sliced
- 1 lb/450 g basmati rice
- 2 cinnamon sticks
- 4 fresh green chiles
- 4 tbsp lemon juice
- 2 tbsp cilantro leaves

Mix the ginger, garlic, garam masala, chili powder, half the salt, the yogurt, and the cardamoms in a bowl. Skin and cut the chicken into 8 pieces, add to the spices, and mix well. Cover and marinate in the refrigerator for 3 hours.

Boil the milk in a small saucepan, pour over the saffron, and set aside. Heat the ghee in a saucepan. Add the onions and cook until golden. Transfer half of the onions and ghee to a bowl and set aside.

Place the rice and cinnamon sticks in a saucepan of water. Bring the rice to a boil and remove from the heat when half-cooked. Drain and place in a bowl. Mix with the remaining salt.

Chop the chiles and set aside. Add the chicken mixture to the pan containing the onions. Add half each of the chopped green chiles, lemon juice, cilantro, and saffron milk. Add the rice, then the rest of the ingredients, including the reserved onions and ghee. Cover tightly. Cook over low heat for 1 hour. Check that the meat is cooked through; if it is not cooked, return to the heat, and cook for an additional 15 minutes. Mix well before serving.